## Wiltshire & Somerset

Edited By Sarah Olivo

First published in Great Britain in 2019 by:

**Young Writers** Est. 1991

Young Writers
Remus House
Coltsfoot Drive
Peterborough
PE2 9BF
Telephone: 01733 890066
Website: www.youngwriters.co.uk

All Rights Reserved
Book Design by Spencer Hart
© Copyright Contributors 2018
SB ISBN 978-1-78988-113-4
Printed and bound in the UK by BookPrintingUK
Website: www.bookprintinguk.com
YB0390F

# Foreword

Dear Reader,

Are you ready to explore the wonderful delights of poetry?

Young Writers' *Poetry Patrol* gang set out to encourage and ignite the imaginations of 5-7 year-olds as they took their first steps into the magical world of poetry. With **Riddling Rabbit**, **Acrostic Croc** and **Sensory Skunk** on hand to help, children were invited to write an acrostic, sense poem or riddle on any theme, from people to places, animals to objects, food to seasons. *Poetry Patrol* is also a great way to introduce children to the use of poetic expression, including onomatopoeia and similes, repetition and metaphors, acting as stepping stones for their future poetic journey.

All of us here at Young Writers believe in the importance of inspiring young children to produce creative writing, including poetry, and we feel that seeing their own poem in print will keep that creative spirit burning brightly and proudly.

We hope you enjoy reading this wonderful collection as much as we enjoyed reading all the entries.

# Contents

**Cleve House School, Knowle**

| | |
|---|---|
| Nathaniel Rhoden (6) | 1 |
| Alex Colton (5) | 2 |
| Frank Gibbons (5) | 3 |
| Thomas (5) | 4 |

**Emersons Green Primary School, Emersons Green**

| | |
|---|---|
| Alisha Shelina Stevens (5) | 5 |
| Eva Hutton (5) | 6 |
| Amberley Cole (5) | 7 |
| Sophie Budd (6) | 8 |
| Penny Ann Bishop (5) | 9 |
| Harry James (5) | 10 |
| Ruby Mae Pyne (6) | 11 |
| Annabelle Hodges (6) | 12 |
| Isaac Rosenberg (5) | 13 |
| Imogen Turner (5) & Violet Pearce | 14 |
| Roseanna Lawrance (6) | 15 |
| Elicie Savage (6) | 16 |
| George Willson (6) | 17 |

**Headley Park Primary School, Headley Park**

| | |
|---|---|
| Noah Ford (6) | 18 |

**Hindhayes Infant School, Street**

| | |
|---|---|
| Noémie Berry (7) | 19 |
| Archie Wall (6) | 20 |
| Henry James Seaward (7) | 21 |
| Faith Nicole Whaites (7) | 22 |
| Logan Mander-James (6) | 23 |

| | |
|---|---|
| Ada Hole (6) | 24 |
| Fletcher Anderton (6) | 25 |

**Hullavington CE Primary School, Hullavington**

| | |
|---|---|
| Jassmine Jessica Watson (6) | 26 |
| Evie Edwards (6) | 27 |
| Oliver Selwood (7) | 28 |
| Amelia Rawlinson (5) | 29 |
| Zoe Cole (6) | 30 |
| Freya Warner (6) | 31 |
| Rosie Anibel Allaway (6) | 32 |
| Poppy Stewart (6) | 33 |
| Ruby Williams (6) | 34 |
| Jonah Michael Raskin (7) | 35 |
| Bella Louise Shaw (7) | 36 |
| Ruby Stocks (5) | 37 |
| Eleftheria (Ellie) Baig (6) | 38 |
| Michael Hope (6) | 39 |

**Moorlands Junior School, Bath**

| | |
|---|---|
| Lyra Edgley (5) | 40 |
| Danielle Madu (6) | 41 |
| Sofia Fox (5) | 42 |
| Matu Cofocanita (5) | 43 |
| M Hadi Hayat (6) | 44 |

**Severn Beach Primary School, Severn Beach**

| | |
|---|---|
| Mason-Lee Withers (6) | 45 |

## Shrewton CE VC Primary School, Shrewton

| | |
|---|---|
| Ethan Holland (5) | 46 |
| Tyler Cain (5) | 47 |
| Eva Maynard (5) | 48 |

## Wroughton Infant School, Wroughton

| | |
|---|---|
| Brooke Tracey (6) | 49 |
| Mabel Ray Mackay (6) | 50 |
| Ella May Norman-Thorpe (6) | 51 |
| Darcey Silto-Baker (6) | 52 |
| Sophie Smith (6) | 53 |
| Ruben Stols (5) | 54 |
| Isabella Walter (7) | 55 |
| Ishbel Spark (6) | 56 |
| Shasmeen Qaddus (6) | 57 |
| Noah Lant (5) | 58 |
| Kieran Paul Gilbert (6) | 59 |
| Elissa Addei (6) | 60 |
| Thomas Parsons (6) | 61 |
| Ellie-May Lee (6) | 62 |
| Maeve Ivie (6) | 63 |
| Isla Louise Young (5) | 64 |
| Charlotte Grace Millwaters (5) | 65 |
| Lily Atkin (6) | 66 |
| Hollie Cooper (6) | 67 |
| Ella Burdell (6) | 68 |
| Georgia Tarling (6) | 69 |
| Louis Arbër Cena (6) | 70 |
| Jack Whitehead (6) | 71 |
| Hayley Krantic Sharma (5) | 72 |
| Leonie Rose (6) | 73 |
| Daisy Cahill (5) | 74 |
| Nathaniel Orion Cottrell (6) | 75 |
| Chloe Mae Humphries (6) | 76 |
| Bramm Walton (6) | 77 |
| Madison Linton (6) | 78 |
| Nicholas Mealing (6) | 79 |
| Teddy Edwards (6) | 80 |
| Albert Raychee Zhang (6) | 81 |
| Arthur Maxwell Mandry (6) | 82 |
| Tomas Carroll (5) | 83 |
| Rupert Forrest Walker (6) | 84 |
| Harry Joseph Wilson (6) | 85 |
| Kobi Mannion (6) | 86 |
| Hugo Hoy (6) | 87 |
| Eloise Small (5) | 88 |
| Elijah Lee Willis (6) | 89 |
| Faith Upton (5) | 90 |
| Tomas Costa (6) | 91 |
| Lauren Frances Ann Waite (6) | 92 |
| Noah Corry (6) | 93 |
| Chloe Peel (6) | 94 |
| Seren Barnes (6) | 95 |
| Raifen David Mulcock (6) | 96 |
| Gabriella Kate Mota (5) | 97 |
| Riley Christopher James Dalton (5) | 98 |
| Jacob Kevin Ackrill (6) | 99 |
| Sam Gough (6) | 100 |
| Montana-Marie Smith (5) | 101 |
| Ryder Purcell (6) | 102 |
| Ellie McCarthy (5) | 103 |
| Joshua Mills (5) | 104 |
| Mollie Mai Speakman (6) | 105 |
| Daisy Boo Randall (7) | 106 |
| Tom Robinson (6) | 107 |
| Leah McKee (5) | 108 |
| Sky Louise Cook (6) | 109 |
| NJ Edward Cato (5) | 110 |
| Samuel Prince (6) | 111 |
| Joseph William Watson (5) | 112 |
| Tamsin Burchell (5) | 113 |
| Chloe May Withington (5) | 114 |
| Albie Mannion (5) | 115 |

# The Poems

# Autumn

Autumn smells of hot chocolate,
Autumn tastes like marshmallows,
Autumn looks like children playing in the leaves,
Autumn feels like relaxing by the fire,
Autumn sounds like fireworks,
Autumn reminds me of leaves falling from trees.

**Nathaniel Rhoden (6)**
Cleve House School, Knowle

# Autumn

Autumn smells of hot dogs on bonfire night,
Autumn tastes like roasted vegetables,
Autumn looks like leaves falling from trees,
Autumn feels cold and icy,
Autumn sounds like apples falling,
Autumn reminds me of the tall trees.

**Alex Colton (5)**
Cleve House School, Knowle

# Autumn

Autumn smells like hot chocolate,
Autumn tastes like pumpkin soup,
Autumn looks like leaves changing,
Autumn feels happy,
Autumn sounds like conkers falling down,
Autumn reminds me of leaves on the football pitch.

**Frank Gibbons (5)**
Cleve House School, Knowle

# Autumn

Autumn smells of warm soup,
Autumn tastes of delicious pie,
Autumn looks like people dressed up,
Autumn feels cold and tasty,
Autumn sounds like people crunching on leaves.

## Thomas (5)
Cleve House School, Knowle

# Chocolate

Chocolate looks shiny like my brown eyes.
Chocolate feels smooth and silky like my brown hair.
Chocolate sounds like a crisp snap when you break it into pieces to share with friends.
Chocolate smells so sweet.
When in my tummy, it melts.
Chocolate tastes delicious and yummy like my mama and dada's cuddles at night.

**Alisha Shelina Stevens (5)**
Emersons Green Primary School, Emersons Green

# Friends

**F** riends like to play
**R** unning about and jumping around
**I** n the forest, playing hide-and-seek
**E** xcited to meet special friends
**N** ew friends of all ages, big and small
**D** ancing, skipping, having fun
**S** it down and watch the show.

## Eva Hutton (5)
Emersons Green Primary School, Emersons Green

# A Frog

**F** rogspawn turns to tadpoles then to frogs.
**"R** ibbit!" says the frog, he jumps around.
**O** range class love to play with a frog.
**G** reen and slimy frog swimming in water.

**Amberley Cole (5)**
Emersons Green Primary School, Emersons Green

# On Holiday

**S** un is burning hot
**U** nder the clear blue sky
**M** ummy puts suncream on me
**M** ake a sandcastle
**E** xciting to jump in the pool
**R** elax on a sunbed in the sun

## Sophie Budd (6)
Emersons Green Primary School, Emersons Green

# Cheeky Monkey

**M** y tail is long and fuzzy,
**O** n the trees I climb,
**N** aughty or nice?
**K** ing of the jungle,
**E** veryone likes playing with me,
**Y** ellow bananas I eat.

**Penny Ann Bishop (5)**
Emersons Green Primary School, Emersons Green

# A Wobbly Creature

I have eight wobbly legs
I can swim
I can hide in rocks
I wobble like jelly
I have tentacles that stick like glue
What am I?

Answer: An octopus.

## Harry James (5)
Emersons Green Primary School, Emersons Green

# Hopping High

I can jump really high.
I have a pouch to put my baby in.
I have furry brown skin.
I live in Australia.
What am I?

Answer: A kangaroo.

## Ruby Mae Pyne (6)
Emersons Green Primary School, Emersons Green

# The White Snow

**S** oft flakes on the floor.
**N** ice white angels that I can make.
**O** nly beautiful Christmas flowers grow.
**W** hat fun I have in the snow!

## Annabelle Hodges (6)
Emersons Green Primary School, Emersons Green

# Slippery Splasher

**F** ins that shimmer
**I** 'm an excellent swimmer
**S** plashing my tail
**H** aving gills, I'm not a whale!

What am I?

## Isaac Rosenberg (5)
Emersons Green Primary School, Emersons Green

# A Swimmer Girl!

I have a long green tail.
I have pink hair.
I have a beautiful face
But the tail of a fish.
What am I?

Answer: A mermaid.

**Imogen Turner (5) & Violet Pearce**
Emersons Green Primary School, Emersons Green

# A Swimming Lady

I have long hair that is pink
and I've got a pretty face
and a body with lovely scales.
What am I?

*Answer: A mermaid.*

## Roseanna Lawrance (6)
Emersons Green Primary School, Emersons Green

# A Swimming Lady

A have a tail.
I live in the sea.
I have beautiful rainbow hair.
What am I?

Answer: A mermaid.

## Elicie Savage (6)
Emersons Green Primary School, Emersons Green

# An Eating Animal

I have sharp, fine gills.
I have a pointy fin.
I eat little fish.
What am I?

Answer: A shark.

## George Willson (6)
Emersons Green Primary School, Emersons Green

# The Zoo

Today I'm going to the zoo,
I'm going to see massive giraffes and monkeys too,
I'm going to the big house to see some ants,
Oh my gosh, they're in my pants!
The flamingos are pink,
And the monkeys stink,
And now I'm going home.

**Noah Ford (6)**
Headley Park Primary School, Headley Park

# Noémie

N - I can see aeroplanes *nyoom!*
O - Oranges like to get squeezed
E - A car goes *eeee!*
M - When I'm hungry, I go, "Mmm!"
I - Ice lolly gets licked, licked, licked
E - My spacesuit goes *eeee!*

**Noémie Berry (7)**
Hindhayes Infant School, Street

# I Like Cake

Cake, it is lovely
it is better than chocolate
it tastes like biscuits and chocolate
mmm!
Cake, yum
in my tummy
right, I will go and eat it!

**Archie Wall (6)**
Hindhayes Infant School, Street

# When You Go Swimming

Swimming is good.
When you jump in, it makes a splash.
Swimming is amazing!
Swimming is good exercise.
The swimming pool is warm and lovely.

**Henry James Seaward (7)**
Hindhayes Infant School, Street

# Smells And Feels

Autumn is about leaves.
Autumn is like a warm bed.
Autumn is loud.
Autumn smells like rain.
Autumn is lovely.
Autumn is colourful.

**Faith Nicole Whaites (7)**
Hindhayes Infant School, Street

## The Cake

The cake is chocolate
and the second cake is jam and chocolate
and the next cake is strawberry and
chocolate and jam!

**Logan Mander-James (6)**
Hindhayes Infant School, Street

# The Curry

Curry sounds bold
Curry tastes chicken-y
Curry feels watery
Curry looks crispy
Curry smells like summer.

## Ada Hole (6)
Hindhayes Infant School, Street

# Sense

Summer is beautiful
Summer smells pretty
Summer is sunny
Summer is colourful
Summer is boiling.

**Fletcher Anderton (6)**
Hindhayes Infant School, Street

# Autumn

Autumn tastes like Yorkshire pudding.
Autumn is cold and you want to wrap up warm in a cosy, fluffy blanket.
Autumn looks like grey clouds and they look rainy sometimes.
Autumn is as cold as ice on your tongue.
Autumn leaves are on the brown branches and are crashing together.
In the bright sky there are some clouds.

## Jassmine Jessica Watson (6)
Hullavington CE Primary School, Hullavington

# Autumn Poem

Autumn is colourful, the leaves are red, brown and yellow
I am going to wrap up in my warm blanket
At Halloween I am going to wear my cat mask and I am going to take my Halloween basket
Autumn is breezy and windy
It blows the leaves off the trees
It blows the grass too
Autumn smells like pumpkin pie.

**Evie Edwards (6)**
Hullavington CE Primary School, Hullavington

# Autumn...

Autumn leaves fall off the trees then they turn into crusty leaves
Autumn sounds like the beautiful birds nesting outside
Autumn tastes like my mum's tasty roast
Autumn feels like I want to wrap up in my blanket, next to the cosy fire
Autumn smells like some fire burning outside.

## Oliver Selwood (7)
Hullavington CE Primary School, Hullavington

# Autumn Fun

Autumn smells like roast dinner with Yorkshire puds
I can see red, yellow and brown leaves gently falling to the ground
I can hear birds singing in the trees
Autumn brings prickly pine cones for me to touch
Autumn tastes like hot dogs on Bonfire Night.

**Amelia Rawlinson (5)**
Hullavington CE Primary School, Hullavington

# Autumn Fun!

From outside I can smell my mum cooking dinner
She is cooking the beef, mashed potatoes, sausages, meatballs and pumpkin pie
I come in from the outside and go upstairs
I am cold so I snuggle with my teddy in bed.

**Zoe Cole (6)**
Hullavington CE Primary School, Hullavington

# Autumn Is...

Autumn smells like rainbow buttons.
Autumn looks like Mrs O'C's pink sparkly dress.
Autumn feels like my cosy, colourful blanket.
Autumn tastes like my mum's Yorkshire pudding.

**Freya Warner (6)**
Hullavington CE Primary School, Hullavington

# Gloomy Autumn

Autumn smells like pumpkin pie
Autumn tastes like a roast dinner
Autumn feels like the trees all breezy
Autumn looks like you're celebrating Halloween
Autumn is a miracle.

**Rosie Anibel Allaway (6)**
Hullavington CE Primary School, Hullavington

# Autumn

Autumn smells like my mum's roast dinner
Autumn feels as cold as an ice cube
Autumn looks like leaves falling off the trees
Autumn tastes like my mum's Yorkshire pudding.

**Poppy Stewart (6)**
Hullavington CE Primary School, Hullavington

# Autumn

Autumn looks like leaves
Autumn smells like my nan's pumpkin pie
Autumn is very chilly
The leaves fall down
Autumn sounds like rainbow fireworks.

**Ruby Williams (6)**
Hullavington CE Primary School, Hullavington

# Fabulous Food

Autumn smells like my mum's food
Autumn tastes like my mum's hot dogs
Autumn looks like a pile of leaves
Autumn looks like a blanket of leaves.

**Jonah Michael Raskin (7)**
Hullavington CE Primary School, Hullavington

# Autumn

Autumn sounds quiet.
Autumn smells like Mummy's roast dinner.
Autumn feels like pumpkin soup.
Autumn looks like Mummy's Yorkshire pudding.

**Bella Louise Shaw (7)**
Hullavington CE Primary School, Hullavington

# Autumn

Autumn smells like an autumn breeze.
Autumn sounds like tweeting birds.
Autumn sounds like crunchy leaves.
Autumn feels like spiky pine cones.

**Ruby Stocks (5)**
Hullavington CE Primary School, Hullavington

# Autumn

Autumn smells like birthday cake
Autumn tastes like chocolate
Autumn looks like Mrs O'Callaghan in a rainbow galaxy dress.

**Eleftheria (Ellie) Baig (6)**
Hullavington CE Primary School, Hullavington

# Autumn

Autumn looks like leaves falling off a tree
Autumn smells like the earth
Autumn sounds like birds tweeting.

**Michael Hope (6)**
Hullavington CE Primary School, Hullavington

# Cow And Horse And Many More

Happy goats sleep on the desert island
Cats sleep in the grass
Cats have fur that is black and white
Dogs walk through the mud extremely pleased
While the owner walks with the lead
The cow drinks the milk
The cow has a baby
They sneak through the long grass quietly
The horse is sleeping and snorting through the grass.

## Lyra Edgley (5)
Moorlands Junior School, Bath

# A Small Creature

I live and move around in a dark or bright environment with no difficulties.
My food comes from the ground and leaves.
I have a lot of places to go without having legs.
What am I?

Answer: A snail.

## Danielle Madu (6)
Moorlands Junior School, Bath

# Socks

One day I went to school
I wore knitted socks
When I walked, the patterns changed into chocolate pictures
Also half blue and white
They felt soggy and wet when it rained
It felt like slime.

**Sofia Fox (5)**
Moorlands Junior School, Bath

# Winter On The Street

Snow outside, snow
Children at play
The flakes fly out
In the winter snow, the kids play
And snowflakes fall down.

## Matu Cofocanita (5)
Moorlands Junior School, Bath

# The Snow

The snow is white
It is soft and light
It falls from the sky
I make a snowman
It's so much fun.

## M Hadi Hayat (6)
Moorlands Junior School, Bath

# Superheroes

**S** is for Spider-Man
**U** p in his web
**P** is for the Penguin, he is an
**E** vil villain
**R** obin saves Batman
**H** is for Hulk, he has
**E** nergy
**R** is for Red Hulk
**O** n the rampage
**E** lastigirl is super
**S** tretchy. I love superheroes!

## Mason-Lee Withers (6)
Severn Beach Primary School, Severn Beach

# Autumn Senses

I can see an apple
It rhymes with dapple.

I can smell smoke
It rhymes with Coke.

I can hear birds twittering
It rhymes with singing.

I can touch a soft berry
It rhymes with ferry.

I can taste blackberry
It rhymes with cherry.

**Ethan Holland (5)**
Shrewton CE VC Primary School, Shrewton

# Rhymes

I can see conkers
It rhymes with bonkers.

I can smell acorns
It rhymes with popcorn.

I can hear fireworks
It rhymes with fireworks.

I can touch spikes
It rhymes with likes.

I can taste juice
It rhymes with loose.

**Tyler Cain (5)**
Shrewton CE VC Primary School, Shrewton

# Autumn Senses

I can see an apple
it rhymes with dapple.
I can smell pumpkins
it rhymes with crunching.
I can hear chopping
it rhymes with bopping.
I can feel blackberries
it rhymes with merry.
I can taste something sour
it rhymes with power.

**Eva Maynard (5)**
Shrewton CE VC Primary School, Shrewton

# The Great Fire Of London

I can see terrifying poisonous smoke from the sky.
I can see horrible, scary fire coming from over there.
I can hear mums and dad shouting, "Oh no!"
I can hear children screaming and crying.
I can smell black, poisonous smoke coming in my lungs.
I can smell disgusting, horrible fire.
I feel worried, anxious.
I feel terrified, frightened.

**Brooke Tracey (6)**
Wroughton Infant School, Wroughton

# The Great Fire Of London

I can see terrifying poisonous smoke entering my lungs.
I can see horrid, terrifying fire demolishing houses!
I can hear people screaming in despair because the fire is destroying their houses so they don't have anywhere to live.
I can smell black, horrible and poisonous smoke approaching my lungs.
I can feel hot, blasting fire as it surrounds me.

**Mabel Ray Mackay (6)**
Wroughton Infant School, Wroughton

# The Great Fire Of London

I can see flaming fire spreading rapidly!
I can hear screaming and little children crying.
There is a lot of noise inside the fire.
I hear crackling flames.
I feel smoke rising from my lungs.
I am scared and frightened.
I smell smoke.
At night, the fire stops.
A girl called Chloe dies because there is smoke in her lungs.

**Ella May Norman-Thorpe (6)**
Wroughton Infant School, Wroughton

# The Great Fire Of London

The Great Fire of London smells like boiling hot wood on houses.
I can see an enormous red, orange, yellow and black fire along the street
and people are running all over the place.
I can hear popping and sizzling fire in the air.
I feel boiling with black, sticky smoke in the air
and if you get too close to it, you will get burnt.

**Darcey Silto-Baker (6)**
Wroughton Infant School, Wroughton

# The Great Fire Of London

The terrifying fire's poisonous smoke is making London die.
It smells like poisonous smoke, choking smoke.
It feels boiling hot, raging hot, sizzling, crackling on your skin.
You can hear people screaming, crying, shouting.
You can see animals running, people running for their lives.

## Sophie Smith (6)
Wroughton Infant School, Wroughton

# A Very Good Autumn

Autumn's very good.
Autumn smells like my mum's hot chocolate.
Autumn's very good.
Autumn looks like colourful blankets.
Autumn's very good.
Autumn tastes like yummy roast dinner.
Autumn's very good.
Autumn reminds me of marshmallows.

**Ruben Stols (5)**
Wroughton Infant School, Wroughton

# The Great Fire Of London

I heard popping, sizzling and screaming
it was not nice to hear.
I smelt dangerous smoke
I was choking a lot, I felt sick.
I could see blazing fire
it was scary to see.
I could also see dangerous smoke.
I could feel the heat
it made me sweaty.

**Isabella Walter (7)**
Wroughton Infant School, Wroughton

# The Great Fire Of London

I can see ferocious smoke climbing up the houses rapidly!
I can hear the crackling flames burning down all of the wooden homes!
I can feel poisonous, smooth smoke in peach lungs!
I can smell disgusting, horrible smoke floating around me, floating around me slowly.

### Ishbel Spark (6)
Wroughton Infant School, Wroughton

# The Great Fire Of London

I hear blazing fire which is popping out of London.
The raging fire is making an awful lot of dust!
The fire smells like choking smoke.
I see buildings on fire and the fire is really hot!
I feel warm, hot smoke and I feel my skin popping up.

**Shasmeen Qaddus (6)**
Wroughton Infant School, Wroughton

# Autumn Is Like...

Autumn smells like hot chocolate
Autumn tastes like my mum's roast dinner
Autumn looks like my mummy's pretty flowers
Autumn feels like my cosy bed
Autumn sounds like my bed being changed
Autumn reminds me of my hot chocolate.

**Noah Lant (5)**
Wroughton Infant School, Wroughton

# The Great Fire Of London

I can see the black, dirty smoke.
I can see the flames.
I can hear the fire fizzing.
I can hear babies crying.
I can smell dirty smoke.
I can smell black, scary smoke.
I can feel boiling fire.
I can feel scary smog.

**Kieran Paul Gilbert (6)**
Wroughton Infant School, Wroughton

# Great Fire Of London

I can see black, disgusting smoke.
I can see people running rapidly!
I can hear babies crying loudly!
I can hear mums and dads shouting, "Oh no!"
I can feel smoke in my lungs.
I can feel poisonous smoke in my mouth.

**Elissa Addei (6)**
Wroughton Infant School, Wroughton

# The Great Fire Of London

I smell crackling fire.
I see people running and houses falling.
I feel shocked because my things are getting destroyed.
I hear sizzling fire.
It reminds me to never turn on my oven again.
I see black smoke and babies crying.

## Thomas Parsons (6)
Wroughton Infant School, Wroughton

# The Great Fire Of London

I can see black, dirty smoke and terrifying, smelly fire!
I can see little children crying!
I can hear grown-ups shouting and screaming!
I can smell black, disgusting smoke!
I feel anxious because there is smelly fire around me!

**Ellie-May Lee (6)**
Wroughton Infant School, Wroughton

# London's Burning

I can see flames floating in the air.
I can hear people screaming out loud.
I can smell bright, hot flames.
I feel frightened because there are flames everywhere around me.
I feel scared because my mum and dad are not with me.

**Maeve Ivie (6)**
Wroughton Infant School, Wroughton

# Autumn Is Like...

Autumn smells like roast potatoes and dead leaves.
Autumn tastes like cookies.
Autumn looks like leaves.
Autumn looks like snow.
Autumn sounds like owls hooting.
Autumn has freezing snow.
Autumn reminds me of cats.

**Isla Louise Young (5)**
Wroughton Infant School, Wroughton

# A Very Good Autumn

Autumn tastes like hot chocolate,
Autumn smells like Mummy's roast potatoes,
Autumn is cold and chilly,
Autumn is freezing,
Autumn has conkers on the ground,
Autumn has squirrels collecting nuts.

**Charlotte Grace Millwaters (5)**
Wroughton Infant School, Wroughton

# The Great Fire Of London

I can see babies and little children crying loudly.
I can hear the blazing, crackling fire spreading swiftly around the city.
I can smell poisonous, disgusting smoke in my lungs.
I feel terrified and shocked.

## Lily Atkin (6)
Wroughton Infant School, Wroughton

# Autumn

Autumn smells like roast marshmallows.
Autumn tastes like hot chocolate.
Autumn looks like smoke.
Autumn feels like my bed.
Autumn sounds like animals sleeping.
Autumn reminds me of snow.

**Hollie Cooper (6)**
Wroughton Infant School, Wroughton

# The Great Fire Of London

I can hear crackling fire.
I can see black smoke.
I can hear people screaming and children crying very loudly.
I feel poisonous smoke drifting down.
I can see brutal, colourful, hot fire.

**Ella Burdell (6)**
Wroughton Infant School, Wroughton

# London's Burning

I can see the hot, crackling fire spreading.
I can hear people crying, people shouting, "Run!"
I can smell the smelly fire entering my lungs.
I can feel the fire and smoke around me.

**Georgia Tarling (6)**
Wroughton Infant School, Wroughton

# The Great Fire Of London

I can hear people screaming and shouting.
I can feel big black smoke on my skin.
I can see the big flaming fire
I can hear the crackling smoke!
I can smell poisonous smoky smoke.

**Louis Arbër Cena (6)**
Wroughton Infant School, Wroughton

# The Great Fire

I smell poisonous smoke everywhere.
The fire feels boiling hot.
I can see a burning hot fire sucking up houses.
I can hear crackling wood from the fire.
I feel smoke in my body.

**Jack Whitehead (6)**
Wroughton Infant School, Wroughton

# Autumn

Autumn is growing flowers.
Autumn is cold and chilly.
Autumn is like my mum's hot dogs.
Autumn is squirrels collecting nuts.
Autumn is like leaves falling off the trees.

**Hayley Krantic Sharma (5)**
Wroughton Infant School, Wroughton

# The Great Fire Of London

The fire smells disgusting, poisonous.
The fire is choking and disgusting.
I can see flames crackling, quickly burning.
I can see flames burning rapidly and it tastes disgusting.

**Leonie Rose (6)**
Wroughton Infant School, Wroughton

# Autumn

Autumn smells like frost
It makes my mummy smile
Autumn looks like pretty leaves
Autumn feels like cobwebs
Autumn sounds like Halloween
Autumn reminds me of ice cream.

**Daisy Cahill (5)**
Wroughton Infant School, Wroughton

# The Great Fire Of London

I feel anxious because the ginormous, deadly fire burnt down my house.
The ridiculous fire is burning down buildings like mad.
I smell choking smoke, horrible fire, crackling houses.

**Nathaniel Orion Cottrell (6)**
Wroughton Infant School, Wroughton

# The Great Fire Of London

I can smell poisonous smoke.
I can feel fire coming closer.
I can hear people screaming.
I can see people running away from the fire.
It reminds me of tornadoes exploding.

**Chloe Mae Humphries (6)**
Wroughton Infant School, Wroughton

# The Great Fire Of London

I can see the crackling, poisonous fire outside
I can feel terrifying, blazing fire
I can smell horrid, scary fire starting in the back
I can feel scary smoke in my lungs.

**Bramm Walton (6)**
Wroughton Infant School, Wroughton

# The Great Fire Of London

The fire smells like dirty dust.
Fire, hot, burning, sizzling.
Really giant, huge fire.
The people feel shocked.
See people running fast, rapidly running.

**Madison Linton (6)**
Wroughton Infant School, Wroughton

# The Great Fire Of London

I can see poisonous smoke.
I can hear blazing, crackling fire.
I can smell terrifying poisonous smoke
that's entering my lungs.
I can feel hot, tiny ashes.

**Nicholas Mealing (6)**
Wroughton Infant School, Wroughton

# The Great Fire Of London

I smell burning smoke.
I hear people screaming and crackling wood.
I see houses burning and people getting into boats.
I feel boiling fire and the hot flames.

**Teddy Edwards (6)**
Wroughton Infant School, Wroughton

# What Is It?

It's something you cannot see.
It's something that pulls you down.
Something that makes you breathe.
What is it?

Answer: Gravity.

**Albert Raychee Zhang (6)**
Wroughton Infant School, Wroughton

# The Great Fire Of London

I can see flames, ashes and smoke.
I can see fire burning.
I can hear people screaming, crying.
I can smell smoke, ashes and fire.
I can feel hot fire.

**Arthur Maxwell Mandry (6)**
Wroughton Infant School, Wroughton

# Autumn Is...

Autumn is leaves falling from the trees
Autumn is cold and there are squirrels climbing trees
All the yummy hot chocolate
Autumn is berries in the trees.

**Tomas Carroll (5)**
Wroughton Infant School, Wroughton

# The Great Fire Of London

I can see bright, blazing smoke.
I can hear people screaming in despair.
I can smell poisonous smoke in the air.
I feel scared, worried and lonely.

**Rupert Forrest Walker (6)**
Wroughton Infant School, Wroughton

# The Great Fire Of London

The fire was dancing, a huge, roasting, hot fire.
The raging fire was crackling, popping, hot.
The people were screaming and crying.
I felt scared.

**Harry Joseph Wilson (6)**
Wroughton Infant School, Wroughton

# The Great Fire Of London

I hear crackling wood, the fire is spreading
I can smell burning fire
It sounds like sizzling fire
I can taste dangerous smoke
I feel warm...

**Kobi Mannion (6)**
Wroughton Infant School, Wroughton

# The Great Fire Of London

I can see dirty, disgusting smoke.
I can hear horrible crackling.
I can smell disgusting, horrible smoke.
I can feel horrible dusty smoke on me.

**Hugo Hoy (6)**
Wroughton Infant School, Wroughton

# Autumn

Autumn smells like dead leaves
Autumn tastes like my mummy's hot chocolate
Autumn looks cold
Autumn reminds me of Amelie's birthday.

## Eloise Small (5)
Wroughton Infant School, Wroughton

# Autumn Time Is...

Autumn time is
seeing squirrels climbing trees.
Autumn time is
leaves falling from trees.
Autumn time is
seeing berries.

**Elijah Lee Willis (6)**
Wroughton Infant School, Wroughton

# Autumn

Autumn is cold and windy.
Autumn is squirrels collecting nuts.
Autumn is leaves falling off trees.
Autumn is berries on the trees.

**Faith Upton (5)**
Wroughton Infant School, Wroughton

# The Great Fire Of London

It makes me feel like a flame.
I can see the red, roaring, yellow fire.
I can taste the poisonous smoke.
It is engulfing houses.

**Tomas Costa (6)**
Wroughton Infant School, Wroughton

# The Great Fire Of London

I see the fire sizzling.
I hear screaming from the people running from the fire.
Poisonous smoke is everywhere.
I'm scared.

**Lauren Frances Ann Waite (6)**
Wroughton Infant School, Wroughton

# The Great Fire Of London

I feel sizzling fire and black smoke.
I see fire spreading across London.
I hear people screaming.
I see fire crushing houses.

**Noah Corry (6)**
Wroughton Infant School, Wroughton

# The Great Fire Of London

I can see people screaming.
I can hear crackly flames.
I can smell black, dusty smoke.
I can feel fire coming near my feet.

**Chloe Peel (6)**
Wroughton Infant School, Wroughton

# The Great Fire Of London

I can see hot, blazing fire on the houses!
I can hear babies screaming.
I can feel the hot, burning smoke coming to my lungs.

**Seren Barnes (6)**
Wroughton Infant School, Wroughton

# The Great Fire Of London

I can see people screaming.
I can hear crackly flames.
I can smell black, dusty smoke.
I can feel the dusty fire.

**Raifen David Mulcock (6)**
Wroughton Infant School, Wroughton

# Autumn

Autumn is cold and windy.
Autumn is a roast dinner.
Autumn is hot chocolate.
Autumn is squirrels eating nuts.

**Gabriella Kate Mota (5)**
Wroughton Infant School, Wroughton

# Autumn Time Is...

Autumn time is hearing that there is a squirrel in the tree.
Autumn time is berries.
Autumn time is yellow leaves.

**Riley Christopher James Dalton (5)**
Wroughton Infant School, Wroughton

# London's Burning

I can see poisonous smoke
I can hear people screaming
I feel shocked and terrified
I can smell poison smoke.

**Jacob Kevin Ackrill (6)**
Wroughton Infant School, Wroughton

# London's Burning

I can see smoke
I can hear badness
I can smell smoke coming into my lungs
I can feel hot, terrifying fire.

**Sam Gough (6)**
Wroughton Infant School, Wroughton

# Autumn

Autumn is orange
Autumn is hot chocolate
Autumn is cold and windy
Autumn is leaves falling from the trees.

**Montana-Marie Smith (5)**
Wroughton Infant School, Wroughton

# The Great Fire Of London

The fire looks scary.
I feel scared.
I hear crackling fire burning crispy wood.
I can smell burning smoke.

**Ryder Purcell (6)**
Wroughton Infant School, Wroughton

# A Very Good Autumn

Autumn smells like my mummy's hot chocolate
Autumn tastes like my roast dinner
Autumn reminds me of my bed.

**Ellie McCarthy (5)**
Wroughton Infant School, Wroughton

# Autumn

Autumn is cold.
Autumn is windy.
Autumn is blowy.
Autumn has conkers on the floor.
Autumn is chilly.

**Joshua Mills (5)**
Wroughton Infant School, Wroughton

# The Great Fire Of London

The fire was popping loudly.
The fire was enormous and it was spreading.
The smoke was dusty and disgusting.

**Mollie Mai Speakman (6)**
Wroughton Infant School, Wroughton

# The Great Fire Of London

I can see fire spreading.
I can hear crackling fire.
I feel sad because people now have nowhere to live.

**Daisy Boo Randall (7)**
Wroughton Infant School, Wroughton

# The Great Fire Of London

I can see hot flames.
I can hear hot, burning smoke.
I can smell hot red smoke.
I feel terrified.

**Tom Robinson (6)**
Wroughton Infant School, Wroughton

# A Very Good Autumn

Autumn smells like dead leaves
Autumn tastes like water
Autumn reminds me of the howling wind.

**Leah McKee (5)**
Wroughton Infant School, Wroughton

# The Great Fire Of London

I hear people screaming
I smell the thick smoke from the fire
I see fire spreading in London.

**Sky Louise Cook (6)**
Wroughton Infant School, Wroughton

# Autumn

Autumn smells of bonfires
Autumn is long nights
Autumn is dark
Autumn is hot dogs.

## NJ Edward Cato (5)
Wroughton Infant School, Wroughton

# Autumn

Autumn smells like rain.
Autumn tastes like hot chocolate.
Autumn looks like magic.

**Samuel Prince (6)**
Wroughton Infant School, Wroughton

# Autumn Time Is...

Autumn time is stepping on leaves
and you can see squirrels
and colourful leaves.

**Joseph William Watson (5)**
Wroughton Infant School, Wroughton

# Autumn Time Is...

Autumn time is
seeing squirrels climb trees.
Autumn time is
falling leaves.

**Tamsin Burchell (5)**
Wroughton Infant School, Wroughton

# Autumn Time Is...

Autumn time is bonfires
Autumn conkers fall off the trees
Autumn time is cold!

**Chloe May Withington (5)**
Wroughton Infant School, Wroughton

# Autumn Time Is...

Autumn time is
yellow leaves
seeing squirrels
twirling leaves.

**Albie Mannion (5)**
Wroughton Infant School, Wroughton

# Young Writers Information

We hope you have enjoyed reading this book – and that you will continue to in the coming years.

If you're a young writer who enjoys reading and creative writing, or the parent of an enthusiastic poet or story writer, do visit our website **www.youngwriters.co.uk**. Here you will find free competitions, workshops and games, as well as recommended reads, a poetry glossary and our blog.

If you would like to order further copies of this book, or any of our other titles, then please give us a call or visit **www.youngwriters.co.uk**.

Young Writers
Remus House
Coltsfoot Drive
Peterborough
PE2 9BF
(01733) 890066
info@youngwriters.co.uk

@YoungWritersUK  @YoungWritersCW